Bibliographic information published by the German National Library:

The German National Library lists this publication in the National Bibliography; detailed bibliographic data are available on the Internet at http://dnb.dnb.de .

Imprint:

Copyright © 2018 GRIN Verlag
Print and binding: Books on Demand GmbH, Norderstedt Germany
ISBN: 9783346063335

This book at GRIN:

https://www.grin.com/document/505657

Issam El Masmodi

The Concept of Race in Toni Morrison's "The Bluest Eye"

GRIN Verlag

GRIN - Your knowledge has value

Since its foundation in 1998, GRIN has specialized in publishing academic texts by students, college teachers and other academics as e-book and printed book. The website www.grin.com is an ideal platform for presenting term papers, final papers, scientific essays, dissertations and specialist books.

Visit us on the internet:

http://www.grin.com/

http://www.facebook.com/grincom

http://www.twitter.com/grin_com

Table of Contents

Introduction

The theme of race is one of the most recurrent and controversial themes in literature. It occupies a huge proportion in the African American literary heritage. Moreover, it is a common theme for almost all the writers of color. The theme of race went through different phases throughout the history of the African American literature. At its early stages especially during the time of slavery, blacks used to write about their experiences as slaves such as Fredrick Douglass's *Narrative of the life of Frederick Douglass*[1]. Douglass' descriptions of the horror of slavery arise feelings of pity in the reader. Throughout the narrative, masters harshly whip and lash their slaves until blood reddens their bodies. They even shoot them in the fields since killing a slave is legal. There is no doubt that slaves are treated this way because they are black and all what is black is regarded as inferior. As time passed by, African American writers were inspired by the nature of their race. They wrote a myriad of literary works. Thus, they reached the mainstream in literature and gained several literary awards. For instance, Toni Morrison is the first African American laureate of the Nobel Prize for literature. She is one of the leading figures of the African American literature.

In her novel *The Bluest Eye*, Morrison's tells the story of a young black girl named Pecola Breedlove who becomes insane by her strong desire to have blue eyes, blonde hair and a white skin. At any rate, the following research paper tends to cover several issues that concern the black race in the light of *The Bluest Eye*. It consists of four major chapters. The first chapter is about the racialization of beauty. In other words, it shows how the notion of beauty is culturally constructed. The white dominant culture creates standards of beauty, which do not allow African Americans to consider themselves as beautiful because of their dark of skin. The second chapter further explains how some of the characters in *The Bluest Eye* long for whiteness because it stands for beauty, purity as well as cleanliness. It also tries to uncover the veil on the issue of whiteness in various fields including the apparatus of the cinema and the American literary canon. The third chapter explores the abusive interactions between black and white characters and shows how a small variation in the color of skin can strike some people of their human nature. It also examines the role of capitalism in giving rise to racism and classism. The fourth and the last chapter examines the issue of internalized racism. That is to say, to what extent all the issues that were mentioned in the previous chapters can affect the psyche of the main characters throughout the novel.

---

[1] Douglass, Frederick. *"Narrative of the life of Frederick Douglass"*. Dover Publications, Inc. 1995

1. Racialized Beauty

The characteristics of beauty are mobile, in the sense that they change with time and place. It is a common knowledge that beauty is one of the qualities that makes people proud of themselves. However, this is not always possible. Sometimes, a hindrance like race, as in the case for Toni Morrison's novel *The Bluest Eye*, does not allow some characters to consider themselves as beautiful. Carmen Gillespie comments, "The novel addresses the social forces that drive understanding and definition of cultural constructs such as beauty, normalcy, family, and sexuality. These constructs are a particular issue for African-American communities that are often excluded from representation."(Gillespie, 2008, p46). This runs in harmony with the postmodern notion of discourse. In his *Archaeology of Knowledge*, Foucault defines discourse as "the general domain of all statements, sometimes as an individualizable group of statements, and sometimes as a regulated practice that accounts for a number of statements" (Foucault quoted by Sara Mills, p 53). Discourse builds its antagonism on binary oppositions for instance black/white, East/West, left/right, men/women and so on. Besides, discourse is a social construct based on language. The construction of discourse may include the examples femininity and racism. Beauty is a central focus in Morrison's novel, *The Bluest Eye*. Besides, it is culturally constructed according to race. Therefore, several non-white characters including Pecola Breedlove, Pauline Breedlove, and Claudia suffer from the racialization of beauty. Thus, they are marginalized and not represented at all.

In the *Encyclopedia of Themes in Literature*, Antonio Maurice Daniels states, "In 'The Bluest Eye', Toni Morrison's first novel, the reader encounters Pecola Breedlove—the protagonist of the novel who has to confront the dominant culture's oppressive standard of beauty." (Daniels, 2010, p797). It seems that beauty is based on oppressive and unfair standards of the dominant culture. In other words, the white culture creates standards of beauty that must be respected in order to measure somebody else's beauty. For example, throughout the world of the novel, everybody agree on the fact that beauty means blue eyes, white skin and blonde hair. Therefore, the protagonist, Pecola Breedlove prays for blue eyes every single night for a whole year: "Each night, without fail, she prayed for blue eyes. Fervently, for a year she had prayed. (*The Bluest Eye, p46*). In her mind, Pecola believes that blue eyes will gain her love, respect and even power. Having blue eyes will make her change the way she sees the world. They will take her pain away from the abhorrent hatred and violence she encounters inside and outside her house.

Because she is black, Pecola Breedlove becomes invisible. The notion of Pecola's invisibility here is quite reminiscent of Ralph Ellison's novel *Invisible Man*[2]. In a prologue to Ellison's *Invisible man,* the narrator emphasizes the fact that he is not a ghost. He is a man of flesh and blood. Yet, he is invisible because people refuse to look at him for the reason that he is black.

---

[2] Ellison, Ralph. *"Invisible man". Prologue.* Random House. 1947

The same thing goes with Pecola Breedlove. Her blackness and ugliness make her invisible in the eye of the beholder. For instance, her classmates and teachers ignore her inside the classroom simply because she is not beautiful or rather, she does not possess the dominant culture's standards of beauty as the following quote shows: "Long hours she sat looking in the mirror, trying to discover the secret of the ugliness, the ugliness that made her ignored or despised at school, by teachers and classmates alike. She was the only member of her class who sat alone at a double desk." (*The Bluest Eye, p45*) Pecola's confrontation with Mr. Yacobowski, a white shopkeeper, is another real example of her invisibility: "At some fixed point in time and space, he senses that he need not waste the effort of a glance."(*The Bluest Eye, p48*) Mr. Yacobowski's refusal to look at Pecola illustrates "the total absence of human recognition" (*The Bluest Eye, p48*) Furthermore, he exemplifies the way whites perceive blacks as unworthy. Her ugliness makes him think that she does not deserve a glance.

At any rate, Pecola Breedlove is not the only one who undergoes the unfair standards of beauty. On the other hand, her mother, Pauline Breedlove, suffers from the racialization of beauty as well "unlike her brothers and sisters, Pauline was not noticed or made to feel special. She attributes this invisibility to a deformed foot that manifests after she steps on a rusty nail at the age of two." (*Gillespie, 2008, p68*). Like Pecola, Pauline's ugliness makes her invisible. When she was two years old, Mrs. Breedlove stepped on a rusty nail, resulting in a deformity that will make her psychologically and physically wounded for the rest of her life "the wound left her with a crooked, archless foot that flopped when she walked… this deformity explained for her many things that would have been incomprehensible." (*The Bluest Eye, p110*). Because of this deformity, Pauline could not easily grasp the standards of beauty, especially when she moves to Ohio. In her book "*Toni Morrison's fiction*", Jan Furman states:

> Pauline's lame foot makes her pitiable and invisible until she marries Cholly. But pleasure in marriage lasts only until she moves from Kentucky to Ohio and confronts northern standards of physical beauty and style. She is despised by snooty black women who snicker at her lameness, her unstraightened hair, and her provincial speech. (*Furman, 1999, p15*)

Pauline's relocation with her husband, Cholly, from Kentucky to Ohio makes her review her own standards of beauty. Apparently, Pauline misses her own people. Besides, she is alienated because things in Ohio are different. Consequently, she must adopt and adapt to the way of life in the north. Her first interaction with some women shows how hard it is to submit to the oppressive standards of beauty in Ohio "Pauline felt uncomfortable with the few black women she met. They were amused by her because she did not straighten her hair. When she tried to make up her face as they did, it came off rather badly" (*The Bluest Eye, p119*). Under these hard circumstances, that distort her self-image, Pauline seeks consolation in the beauty of the Fisher's house as a servant "eventually, Pauline gives up on her own family and takes refuge in the soft beauty surrounding her in the Fisher home." (*Furman, 1999, p16*). For Pauline, the Fisher's house is a haven. It keeps her safe from the world outside and her husband in particular. Therefore, she gives up on her family and prefers to serve the Fishers instead. Pauline could not manage to have new friends with a common understanding in such a new environment. Therefore, she eventually surrenders to the standards of beauty: "Money became the focus of all their discussions, hers for clothes, his for drink. The sad thing was that Pauline did not really care for clothes and makeup. She merely wanted other women to cast favorable glances her way." (The Bluest Eye, p118). Her interest in money, clothes and make up demonstrates Pauline's submission to the standards of beauty. She really wants to draw the attention of others.

Unlike Pecola and Pauline, Claudia rejects the white dominant's standards of beauty. She is a symbol of rejection. She rises against racialized beauty on behalf of the African American women: "The primary narrator of the novel, Claudia stands in distinct contrast to Pecola and Pauline. Rather than coveting the blue-eyed, blonde-haired white baby dolls that she receives every Christmas without asking or wanting, Claudia harbors a desire to dismember them." (*Nerad, 2006, p98*) This quote illustrates how Claudia refuses to obey the standards of beauty while other characters rejoice them. Claudia hates the white baby doll she receives for Christmas. She does not understand why others find it charming. For her, the white doll is ugly. Moreover, Claudia destroys the baby doll since nobody asks her what she wants for Christmas: "I did not know why I destroyed those dolls. But I did know that nobody ever asked me what I wanted for Christmas." (*The Bluest Eye, p21*) Claudia tears apart the white doll. By doing so, she refuses the distorted images that the white dominant culture draws about beauty. Therefore, she celebrates her own beauty: "Claudia, whose voice closes the novel, cannot see Pecola's blue eyes but does finally understand that Pecola is 'all the beauty of the world.' Claudia thus rejects the white stereotype of beauty and celebrates her own embodied identity as a young black woman." (*Nerad, 2006, p98*) At the end of the novel, Claudia seems happy with her own beauty. She compares herself with the sad ending of Pecola's life. Subsequently, she finds herself less ugly than Pecola. Ironically, she is luckier than Pecola. She does not end up mentally crazy because of the oppressive standards of beauty: "And all of our beauty, which was hers first and which she gave to us. All of us—all who knew her—felt so wholesome after we cleaned ourselves on her. We were so beautiful when we stood astride her ugliness." (*The Bluest Eye, p205*) Claudia finds beauty in Pecola's ugliness. Due to that, the racialized beauty no longer enslaves her. She liberates herself from the ideas that the white world impose on blacks. Claudia exemplifies the celebration of the black body.

The African American literature is very rich when it comes to the celebration of black beauty. Since the dominant culture neglects and marginalizes the African American women from the realm of beauty, black women writers decided to reconstruct the concept of beauty by taking into consideration their special black features (Olson, p.51). In fact, throughout the history of the African American literature, several black female poets wrote inspirational poems for black women especially Gwendolyn Brooks and Maya Angelou.

Bloom suggests that Gwendolyn Brooks' poem *To Those of My sisters Who Kept Their Naturals* and Toni Morrison's novel "*The Bluest Eye*" deal with the same issue that is the racialization of beauty:

> You have not bought Blondine.
> You have not hailed the hot-comb recently.
> You never worshipped Marilyn Monroe.

You say: Farrah's hair is hers.
You have not wanted to be white
(Gwendolyn quoted by Bloom, p. 15)

Bloom claims that in this extract from *To Those of My sisters who kept Their Naturals* poem, Gwendolyn Brooks praises and encourages African American women for the reason that they resist the widespread notion of beauty in the American media, advertising and movies.

The African American poet, Maya Angelou, is also one of the black female writers who highly praises black beauty. The theme of black beauty's pride predominates much of Angelou's verse and prose volumes. Throughout her poems, she tries to neutralize the white standards of beauty and celebrates her own African American features (Olson, p. 51). For instance, in her *Phenomenal Woman*, Maya Angelou writes:

Pretty women wonder where my secret lies.
I'm not cute or built to suit a fashion model's size
But when I start to tell them,
They think I'm telling lies.
That's me.
(Angelou, p. 130)

Throughout the poem, Angelou reveals her own secrets of beauty. The first four opening verses illustrate the white world stereotypes about beauty. Then, Angelou challenges those stereotypes by celebrating her own black features. Angelou's poems embody powerful images of black beauty. For example, when she says in her poem *Black Ode*, "Your beauty is a thunder" (Angelou, p41) Angelou tries to convince black women that they are naturally beautiful. Moreover, she shows them that the power of black beauty is unconquerable.

Apart from poetry, multiple slogans and movements emerged, as a reaction to the racialization of beauty such as *Black is Beautiful* slogan and the Afrocentric movement. In her essay, *The Bluest Eye and Sula: black female experience from childhood to womanhood* Agnes Suranyi writes: "even though the setting for the story is 1940–41 – the beginning of World War II for the United States – it is also "presentist" in concept, ideologically grounded in the 1960s when "Black is Beautiful" entered into the popular, if more militant, discourse." (*Agnes, 2007, p11*). In this way, the novel views the past with a present-day perspective. The real meanings of *Black is Beautiful* slogan are relevant to the novel. The slogan tried to hearten the black community particularly women to be proud of their dark skin, curly hair and thick lips. Although many black people used the catchphrase, *Black is Beautiful*; it was not associated with any political movement. (Craig, p. 23). On the other hand, the Afrocentric movement sprang out from Africa and soon it inspired the African American community in the 1980's and 1990's. The Afrocentric movement focused on the African and African American cultural legacy. By doing so, the Afrocentric movement challenged Eurocentrism. Besides, the Afrocentric movement took into account black beauty. For instance, new hairstyles came into appearance such as dreadlocks, braids and naturals (Knight, pp. 41/42).

2. Whiteness

Throughout the world of the novel, numerous characters have a predilection for whiteness including Pecola Breedlove, Geraldine, as well as Pauline Breedlove. Their obsession with whiteness explains that the white color as opposed to black stands for purity, cleanliness, and beauty. Morrison exposes this tendency to whiteness from the very beginning of *The Bluest Eye*. Morrison uses and abuses the postmodern technique of intertexuality to dismantle the problematic of whiteness.

Julia Kristiva coined the term Interxtuality in order to indicate that a text is not self-contained and autonomous but rather it is a product of other texts. She claims that there is a network relationship between texts. In this way, the meaning of a particular text depends on other previous texts. The Bulgarian literary theorist and psychoanalyst Julia Kristiva came into appearance in Paris as the interpreter of the Russian Formalist, Mikhail Bakhtin. In his collected essays *The Dialogic Imagination*, Bakhtin refers to the novel as dialogic because it contains a multiplicity of voices, Heteroglossia. In this way, a novel is not fixed as other forms of literature but rather it is subjected to change because it possess parodies, travesties, and reaccentuates (Edgar and Sedgwick. p. 14). Barthes develops the term of Interxtuality in his famous essay *The Death of the Author*. Influenced by Kristeva's work on Bakhtin, Barthes develops the idea of the text as a non-unified authorial consciousness and a form of plurality of quotations of other words, other utterances and other previous texts. As Roland Barthes puts it himself, a text is a "tissue of quotations drawn from the innumerable centers of culture." (Barthes, 146). Morrison starts her first novel by the following intertext taken from an American curriculum:

> Here is the house. It is green and white. It has a red door. It is very pretty. Here is the family. Mother, Father, Dick, and Jane live in the green-and-white house. They are very happy. See Jane. She has a red dress. She wants to play. Who will play with Jane? See the cat. It goes meow-meow. Come and play. Come play with Jane. The kitten will not play. See Mother. Mother is very nice. Mother, will you play with Jane? Mother laughs. Laugh, Mother, laugh. See Father. He is big and strong. Father, will you play with Jane? Father is smiling. Smile, Father, smile. See the dog. Bowwow goes the dog. Do you want to play with Jane? See the dog run. Run, dog, run. Look, look. Here comes a friend. The friend will play with Jane. They will play a good game. Play, Jane, play. (*The Bluest Eye*)

The intertext from the *Dick and Jane* curriculum is very significant to understand the issue of whiteness in *The Bluest Eye*. The reader anticipates the unfolding of the novel through a white lens. While reading the epigraph, it sounds as if someone says this is whiteness. It is very pretty, clean, and happy. Moreover, the epigraph provides the reader with an ideal white family. The family consists of father, mother, Dick and Jane, living in a pretty house. In each section of the novel, Morrison starts with a sentence from the epigraph to tell the story of a particular character. By doing so, Morrison uses the epigraph as a juxtaposition in order to compare whiteness with blackness. Linden Peach comments on the use of the Dick and Jane primer "the text brings a particular perspective not only to the impact of white ideologies on the black community, but also to the nature of whiteness and its inappropriateness to determine the contours of African-American culture and lived experience. (*Peach, 1995, p38*). This shows how the white world and its ideologies are unable to represent the contours of the black world. Besides, the epigraph is a testimony of the idealized whiteness. Thus, blackness is marginalized from the beginning of the novel as Rachel Lister states "the threat of marginalization haunts The Bluest Eye from the beginning. Morrison opens the novel with a generic narrative that will be familiar to many readers: the first words of a child's primer, introducing the members of a white family. (*Lister, 2009, p26*).

Next to the marginalization of blackness, the extract from Dick and Jane primer is repeated twice. Morrison repeats the first one without punctuation and the last one with no spacing. By doing so, Morrison illustrates that there is a lack of order in the black world. "The order of the white world, its coherence and moral certainty, is juxtaposed throughout with the disunity and search for coherence in the lives of the African-Americans." (*Peach, 1995, p35*). This disorder will lead many characters to be fond of whiteness.

To start with, Pecola is the first victim of these white ideologies and this lack of coherence. Once when was dwelling with the Macteers, Pecola drunk a huge amount of milk. Mrs. Macteer comments angrily on Pecola's act: "Three quarts of milk. That's what was in that icebox yesterday. Three whole quarts. Now they ain't none. Not a drop. I don't mind folks coming in and getting what they want, but three quarts of milk! What the devil does anybody need with three quarts of milk? (*The Bluest Eye, p23*). The act of drinking three quarts of milk illustrates Pecola's strong obsession with whiteness. In her mind, Pecola believes that if she drinks milk, she will consequently white. She even drinks milk from a cup of Shirley Temple, a white American child movie star. In an article about *Whiteness*, David E. Magill states, "Morrison constantly portrays whiteness as a property, a commodity with value that implicitly marks Blackness as having no value." (*Magill, 2003, p377*). According to Magill, Morrison portrays blackness as invaluable. Besides, whiteness in Toni Morrison's works is like a commodity. Thus, metaphorically speaking, Pecola always strives to buy whiteness.

Geraldine, a multiracial character, is one of the other characters who longs for whiteness as well. This can be explained by the fact that "multiracial characters provide one means for Morrison to destabilize whiteness. The logic of whiteness depends on a binary notion of race rooted in unequal difference... Their unstable racial identity undermines the strict logic of binary difference that supports white superiority" (*Magill, 2003, p378*). It is obvious that the presence of multiracial characters such as Geraldine, Maureen Peal as well as Soaphead Church makes the issue of whiteness much complicated. In a way or another, these characters try to neglect their African American roots, for the reason that blackness stands for dirtiness. Therefore, they take refuge in whiteness.

Jan Furman shows how Geraldine distinguishes niggers from colored people: "When Pecola stands in Geraldine's house–tricked there by Geraldine's hateful son–she transgresses a line demarking "colored people" from "niggers" (*Furman, 1996, p15*). Geraldine tells her son that niggers are dirty and loud whereas colored people are neat and quiet. By doing so, she draws a line between black and white. The more someone approaches to the white color the more he or she becomes clean as the following quote shows "his mother did not like him to play with niggers. She had explained to him the difference between colored people and niggers. They were easily identifiable. Colored people were neat and quiet; niggers were dirty and loud" (*The Bluest Eye, p87*).

In his essay *Toni Morrison's 'Allegory of the cave': Movies, consumption, and Platonic Realism in The Bluest Eye*, Thomas H. Fick states, "Movies are the centrally destructive force in the novel not only because of the values they present—perfect white bodies and romantic love—but because of the way they present them" (*Fick, 2007, p20*). Hollywood as a cinematic device plays a major role in disseminating the ideals of whiteness in *The Bluest Eye*. Moreover, the cinema targets the minds and psyches of various characters. In this vein, the cinema is major component of Althusser's the ideological state apparatus because it maintains the ideology of the ruling class (Edgar and Sedgwick. p. 5). Throughout the novel, Morrison refers to multiple white movie stars:

> The MacTeers's boarder, Mr. Henry, delights in calling the young girls Greta Garbo and Ginger Rogers; Pecola drinks three quarts of milk just to see Shirley Temple's picture on the mug; black women have their hair styled like Hedy Lamarr's; Betty Grable's name looms large on theatre marquees. (*Fick, 2007, p24*)

When Mr. Henry, The Macteers' new dweller, enters the house, he greets Frieda and her sister, Claudia as follows, "Hello there. You must be Greta Garbo, and you must be Ginger Rogers." (The Bluest Eye, p16). By associating Frieda and Claudia to the white actresses, Ginger Rogers and Greta Garbo, Morrison shows how black men are preoccupied by white movie stars. Another instance in which black characters refer to white actresses is when Maureen Peal, Pecola, Claudia and Frieda were walking back home from school. They passed by Dreamland Theater where they saw a picture of Betty Grable smiling down at them, "We passed the Dreamland Theater, and Betty Grable smiled down at us. 'Don't you just love her?' Maureen asked. 'Uh-huh,' said Pecola. I differed. 'Hedy Lamarr is better'. (*The Bluest Eye, p69*).

Pauline Breedlove is the most affected character of the white ideologies that the cinema propagandizes, "Pauline Breedlove is the cinema's primary victim, and her story gives shape and context to Pecola's more general tragedy." (*Fick, 2007, p24*). The world of the cinema is the second hideaway for Pauline after the house of the Fishers. Inside the walls of the theater, Pauline compares her ugliness with the white reflection of the images on the screen as Gena Elise Chandler comments, "She becomes enamored with white movie starlets and resigns herself to ugliness in the face of what is simply her difference… she chooses to see only ugliness. Transferring her desires to reflect the white images on the screen. (*Chandler, 2003, p74*). There is no doubt that the cinema exercises a huge impact on Pauline. In the first place, she names her daughter Pecola after a movie: "Pauline is enamored of Hollywood films and may have gotten her daughter's name from the character Peola in the 1934 version of the movie "Imitation of Life" (*Gillespie, 2008, p68*). The second example is when Pauline speaks to herself through a monologue, "I 'member one time I went to see Clark Gable and Jean Harlow. I fixed my hair up like I'd seen hers on a magazine." (*The Bluest Eye, p123*). The way she styles her hair like a white movie actress is another manifestation of the cinema's influence on Pauline.

The issue of whiteness is still relevant nowadays. In an article about *Whiteness*, Sharon Jesse writes, "the study of whiteness has become a focus of mainstream scholarship and the popular press. The central emphasis of recent scholarship is making visible the signs of white identity" (*Jesse, 2006, p901*). Several scholars focus on the study of whiteness in the contemporary era. For instance, Rachel Lister talks about a documentary that the postcolonial critic, Henry Louis Gates Jr., did in 2003 under the title of *America beyond the Color Line*. In his documentary, Gates visits Los Angeles in order to examine the issue of race in Hollywood's films industry. Gates came up with the following:

> Speaking to black actresses, Gates found that the industry continues to cast lighter-skinned over darker-skinned actresses. When he addresses the issue of what he terms "one of Hollywood's darkest secrets: the colorline within the race," he finds that "small variations in skin tone canmake or break a black woman's career. (*Lister, 2009, p82*)

Whiteness stands also in relation to the Christian creed in novel. In his essay, *The Fourth Face: The Image of God in Toni Morrison's The Bluest Eye*, Allen Alexander states,

> Religious references, both from Western and African sources, abound in Toni Morrison's fiction, but nowhere are they more intriguing or perplexing than in 'The Bluest Eye'. And of the many fascinating religious references in this novel, the most complex—and perhaps, therefore, the richest—are her representations of and allusions to God. (*Alexander, 2007, p111*)

Throughout *The Bluest Eye*, Morrison reveals a very controversial and sensitive issue that is the whiteness of God. Through the character of Cholly, Morrison states, "He wondered if God looked like that. No. God was a nice old white man, with long white hair, flowing white beard, and little blue eyes that looked sad when people died and mean when they bad it must be the devil who looks like that" (*The Bluest Eye, p134*). Once on the Fourth of July, Cholly and his friend, Blue Jack, went for a walk. While the father of one of the families was raising a watermelon over his head ready to smash it on the floor, Cholly looked up at his long arm and wondered if God looked like that man. However, Cholly figured out later that God was a nice old white man with long white hair. Therefore, the man must resemble the devil. By doing so, Morrison ironically associates whiteness with God and blackness with evil. Secondly, When Geraldine tells Pecola to get out of her house; Pecola turns to find the front door and sees Jesus looking down at her. Pecola waits for Jesus to interfere and do something. However, he seems helpless, "Pecola turned to find the front door and saw Jesus looking down at her with sad and unsurprised eyes, his long brown hair parted in the middle, the gay paper flowers twisted around his face. *(The Bluest Eye, p92-93)*.

The statue of Jesus Christ appears as a black figure in multiple occasions on the screen. For instance, the famous pop singer, Madonna. In her video clip, *Like a Prayer*[3], a man appears as a black Jesus statue who comes to life and kisses Madonna on her forehead. The American comedy television series, *Black Jesus*[4] by Aaron McGruder and Mike Clattenburg, is another example of the portrayal of Jesus as black. The series feature a black Jesus Christ living in Compton, California. His mission is to spread love and kindness throughout the neighborhood. In an article titled *What's wrong with Black Jesus?*, the American author, Jay Parini, comments on the series, "It appears that nobody is quite sure whether this is a madman who thinks he is Jesus or maybe the lord himself come back in a strange outfit and, indeed, black skin." (Parini, 2014). From this comment, it becomes obvious that the appearance of Jesus as a black holy figure on the screen brings so much controversy. In an introduction titled *The Holy Face of Race* from their book *The Color of Christ: The Son of God and the Saga of race in America*", Edward J. Blum and Paul Harvey state:

> Jesus changed shape as a white figure in the United States because who was considered white and what being white meant have mutated over time. The parameters of who was deemed white, what their whiteness meant, and how it was connected to citizenship rights have shifted, sometimes dramatically, sometimes delicately, throughout American history. Whiteness as a category of identity and as a marker for privilege has been created, tested, and transformed repeatedly, and white Jesus figures have been reworked to fit the varied circumstances. *(Blum and Harvey, 2012, p7)*

The representation of Jesus changes over time. Throughout the American history, Americans have drawn different sketches of Jesus for their own benefits. Furthermore, the whiteness of Jesus serves as a metaphor of white supremacy. The white Jesus marginalizes black Christians. He does not represent them. Consequently, Jesus takes the shape of a black holy figure in different forms of art in order to challenge racism in different forms of art.

> At other times, religious ideas and images challenged racism, whether in the form of novelist Harriet Beecher Stowe imagining a whipped slave as she took communion and then writing 'Uncle Tom's Cabin' or of artists painting new black, red, or brown portraits of Jesus to inspire pride in peoples rendered nonwhite. *(Blum and Harvey, 2012, p16)*

The issue of whiteness is omnipresent in the American literary canon as well. Moreover, whiteness has become an ideology rather an identity in multiple canonical works including Herman Melville's *Moby Dick* as Harold Bloom states:

---

[3] Madonna. *Like a Prayer*. YouTube, 26. Oct. 2006,
<http ://www.youtube.com/watch?v=79fzeNUqQbQ>
[4] McGruder, Aaron, and Clattenburg, Mike. *Black Jesus*. Imdb, 7. Aug. 2014.

Toni Morrison, in a speculative essay on literary canon-making, proposes the difficult critical quest of uncovering the hidden obsession with African-Americans that has haunted the American novel throughout its history. Her principal example is to sketch a reading of 'Moby-Dick' in which Ahab's manic obsessiveness with the whiteness of the whale becomes a synecdoche for white America's compulsive relation to the African-American aspects of its culture, past and present. *(Bloom, 2005, p1)*

Morrison examines the issue of whiteness many times in her writings. Bloom claims that in Morrison's reading to Herman Melville's masterpiece *Moby Dick*, she finds out that Ahab's obsession for the whiteness of the whale has become a synecdoche for both white and black America's connections as a whole. Furthermore, Ahab obsession with the whiteness of the whale interprets the superiority of the white race over the other races within the American community. Moreover, in her critical work *Playing in the Dark: Whiteness and the literary Imagination*, Morrison explores the presence of blackness or what she calls "American Africanism" in the American literary canon. Throughout her readings to several American writers such as Edgar Allan Poe, Willa Cather, Mark Twain, Ernest Hemingway and others, Morrison discovers that their works feature blackness. Moreover, they even depict black people with negative connotations in their works. (Morrison, 1993)

3. Everyday Racism

Race and racism are two confusing terms. However, they are not interchangeable. In *The World Book Encyclopedia,* Stanley M. Garn suggests, "Race has been used as a major basis of telling one group from another." *(Garn, 1985, p50).* Race plays a major role in differentiating one human race from another. There are various human races all over the world. Therefore, it becomes hard to classify some people into their original races especially if they are from the same race. John Hartwell Moore further explains the diversity of races among species, "A race, then, might represent a minor adaptation to local conditions within the species. A species of butterflies, for example, might include "races" which present different patterns of camouflage on their wing" *(Moore, 2008, pXI).* Sometimes, some people misunderstand the term of race. Therefore, they use it as a mean of prejudice and superiority as Stanley M. Garn states:

> The idea of race has often been misunderstood, and the term has sometimes been misused on purpose. Race has often confused with culture, language, nationality, or religion. Differences in physical appearance have led some people to mistakenly conclude that members of some races are born with superior intelligence, talents, and moral standards. Race has also been a major basis of racial discrimination by one group against the other. *(Garn, 1985, p51-52)*

There is a gap between race and racism. When the idea of race is misunderstood, it gives rise to racism. Therefore, race should not be mixed with other terms such as intelligence, nationality, and culture as a whole. In the first chapter, *"Race" fact or artifact?* from his book *"Race" and Racism: The Development of Modern Racism in America* Richard J. Perry: states: "Racism is a cultural artifact, the product of a particular cultural context—a part of a belief system." *(Perry, 2007 p: 2)*. Unlike race, people make racism. That is to say, it is culturally constructed. Besides, the belief of racism has led many people to commit multiple inhuman acts throughout history such as the genocide of the Jews by Hitler under the pretext of belonging to the superior Nordic race. *(Pettigrew, 1985, p61)*.

There is no doubt that racism is one of the biggest issues in the history of humanity. The unfair ideologies of racism have led many people to suffer from racial discrimination, violence and other unfair racial deeds. Racism has in particular deep roots in the history of the United States of America starting from the time of slavery onward: "In 1903, the African-American writer W. E. B. DuBois suggested that the biggest problem of the 20th century would be the problem of race." *(Emery, 2011, p85)* W.E.B DuBois' famous prophetic saying foretells the American racist ideologies that *The Bluest Eye* tries to deal with.

At any rate, throughout the novel, many black characters are mistreated and even dehumanized by whites because of their skin color including Cholly Breedlove, Pecola Breedlove as well as Pauline Breedlove. First, Cholly's encounter with two white hunters is one of the most humiliating racial acts in the novel,

> When he was still very young, Cholly had been surprised in some bushes by two white men while he was newly but earnestly engaged in eliciting sexual pleasure from a little country girl. The men had shone a flashlight right on his behind. He had stopped, terrified. They chuckled. The beam of the flashlight did not move. "Go on," they said. "Go on and finish. And, nigger, make it good. *(The Bluest Eye, p42)*

After the funeral of Aunt Jimmy, Cholly, Darlene, Jake, and Suky decided to go for a walk. While Cholly and Darlene were having fun, two white hunters appeared with their flashlight in the dark. Then, they ordered Cholly and Darlene to continue performing what they were doing. The white hunters roughly insulted Cholly and Darlene, "Cholly's first sexual experience was shared under the glaring lights and eyes of two white hunters who stumbled upon Cholly and then forced him to finish the sex act under their watchful glare. Since that day, Cholly has struck back at the white world that humiliated him *(Chandler, 2003, p73)*. Cholly's experience with the white hunters had a deep impact on him. Therefore, he changed the way he used to see white people. The white hunters' hatred and oppression caused Cholly to be a cruel and harsh man especially with his family.

On the other hand, Pecola Breedlove was racially abused from different characters in the novel particularly by the character of Yacobowski. The latter "reaches over and takes the pennies from her hand. His nails graze her damp palm. *(The Bluest Eye, p49-50)*. Aside from Pecola's invisibility to Mr. Yacobowski, he harshly scratches her hand with his nails. This abusive act demonstrates the intense dislike that Mr. Yacobowski feels toward black people.

Moreover, it shows the cruel nature of racism. Secondly, when Louis Junior, Geraldine son, invites Pecola to his house in order to see his mother's kittens, he throws a black cat on Pecola's face. Thus, the cat tears at Pecola's face and chest with its nails, "He threw a big black cat right in her face. She sucked in her breath in fear and surprise and felt fur in her mouth. The cat clawed her face and chest in an effort to right itself, then leaped nimbly to the floor. *(The Bluest Eye, p89-90)*. The act of throwing the cat on Pecola's face illustrates Louis Junior's disgust toward black children. His mother taught him to hate black children and she did not allow him to play with them because they were dirty. Therefore, Louis Junior's racial act is based on Pecola's dark skin. Louis Junior does not bother black girls for the reason that he fears they would beat him up. Moreover, Louis Junior regards black girls as animals in saying, "they usually traveled in packs" *(The Bluest Eye, p: 87)*. He compares the gathering of the black girls to a group of hunting animals through a metaphor. By doing so, Morrison shows how a small variation in skin color can strikes blacks from their human nature. The interaction between Pauline Breedlove and a white doctor in the hospital is another example of depicting blacks as animals, "When he got to me he said now these here women you don't have any trouble with. They deliver right away and with no pain. Just like horses. *(The Bluest Eye, p124-125)*. The old doctor harshly dehumanizes Pauline. He makes the young doctors laugh at her by comparing her to a horse. By doing so, Morrison tries to show to the reader particularly whites that black women feel the same pain while giving birth to a baby just like the rest of women. Moreover, Morrison reveals the bad effects of racial discrimination on blacks. For instance, the doctors do not treat blacks as equal as whites, "I weren't no horse foaling. But them others. They didn't know. They went on. I seed them talking to them white women: 'How you feel? Gonna have twins?' Just shucking them, of course, but nice talk. Nice friendly talk. *(The Bluest Eye, p125)*.

Through the character of Soaphead Church, Morrison shows how colored people advocate and even encourage the white racist ideologies. Even though he has African American roots, Soaphead Church is very proud of his British ancestors. Besides, his ancestors transferred of what Morrison calls "Anglophilia" *(The Bluest Eye, p: 168)* from father to son. Therefore, they believed in the superiority of the white race,

> With the confidence born of a conviction of superiority, they performed well at schools. They were industrious, orderly, and energetic, hoping to prove beyond a doubt De Gobineau's hypothesis that "all civilizations derive from the white race, that none can exist without its help, and that a society is great and brilliant only so far as it preserves the blood of the noble group that created it. *(The Bluest Eye, p168)*

Soaphead Church does not only agree with De Gobineau's hypothesis but he even proves it right. John Hartwell Moore states: "the persons who invented racism were themselves members of the race that they alleged was superior—the white race—Nordic and European. Carolus Linnaeus (1707–1778), Johan Blumenbach (1752–1840), and Arthur de Gobineau (1816–1882)" *(Moore, 2008, pXI)*. Morrison refers to one the inventors of racism, De Gobineau. The latter was a member of the race he asserted to be superior that is the white race.

In her essay, *On Class Versus Race as a Cause of Black Oppression,* Doreatha Drummond Mbalia writes, "Morrison is conscious of the role economics plays in the African's having a wholesome self-image. For it is the Breedloves' fight for survival that weakens the family structure and makes the family members more vulnerable to the propaganda of the dominant culture." *(Mbalia, 2010, p92)* Morrison is aware about the role that social class plays in the novel. For example, The Breedloves are the most influenced family members to the ideals of the dominant culture because of their social class as Morrison states: "The Breedloves did not live in a storefront because they were having temporary difficulty adjusting to the cutbacks at the plant. They lived there because they were poor and black." *(The Bluest Eye, p38).* The Breedloves were ugly for the reason that they were poor and black. Therefore, race as well as social class determine one's beauty and ugliness.

> The Bluest Eye' explores the theme of outdoors as it exposes the vulnerability of the community depicted in the novel. Subjected to the whims of racism and classism, particularly potent in the post-Depression 1930s and early 1940s, the people of Lorain have to work hard to ensure that their existence is secure. Their actions are often controlled by their legitimate fear of being displaced, of losing the central marker of stability and identity, the house. *(Gillespie, 2008 p54)*

The setting of the novel explains the displacement and poverty of the Breedloves. *The Bluest Eye* takes place after the Great Depression. John Steinbeck's *The Grapes of Wrath* better illustrates the spirit of America at that time because of the decline of the economy that has led many people to suffer financially. The causalities of the Great Depression make the Breedloves suffer from poverty as well as racial discrimination. Moreover, the variation in social classes results in racism as well as classism. That is to say, an exploitative economical system produces racist ideologies,

> Class exploitation is perhaps the greatest source of oppression of blacks in White America. The class issue is an important one as it is linked to Capitalism, the system which divides society into two classes: 'master' and 'slaves.' The whites have been the Monopoly Class under this system while the blacks have been the Marginal Class *(Bharati and Joshi, 2009, p38)*

The exploitative economical system divides the world of the novel into two classes. First, the upper class that manipulates the economic system. Secondly, the lower class that is marginalized and has low incomes. Morrison depicts these two social classes in the novel through the Dick and Jane family, the Macteers as well as the Breedloves: "Here is the house. It is green and white. It has a red door. It is very pretty. Here is the family. Mother, Father, Dick, and Jane live in the green-and-white house. They are very happy." *(The Bluest Eye).* Morrison starts her novel by exposing to the reader a white bourgeoisie family from the Dick and Jane primer. By doing so, Morrison shows that the white capitalist families live in luxury due to the exploitation of the economy whereas black poor families such as the Breedloves and the Macteers live in bad conditions. In the end of her, essay *On Class Versus Race as a Cause of Black Oppression,* Mbalia states:

It is interesting to note that just as Africans in the United States in the 1960s and early 1970s viewed the primary enemy of African people as "the white man," so does Morrison, writing 'The Bluest Eye' in the late 1960s, see the issue as one of European versus African. However, as she continues to think about, write about, and experience the ongoing oppression of African people despite the gains of the Civil Rights Movement, she will become more conscious of the fact that capitalism, not racism, is the African's greatest enemy. *(Mbalia, 2010, p96)*

Mbalia concludes her essay with the idea that racism is not the only monster that haunts black people; capitalism remains the main enemy for the African American community.

4. Internalized Racism

Morrison's *The Bluest Eye* is the first full-length work that will focus on the issue of internalized racism. Panlay states, "As a theme, internalized racism has always been explored or treated, though 'peripherally', Toni Morrison's first novel, The Bluest Eye (1999), an adult book focalized through a child narrator, is arguably the first full-length novel that puts this racial issue at the center" *(Panlay, 2016, p2)*. Morrison is conscious about the outcome of racism and all the issues that are related to the black race on the psyche of the African American community. The way Morrison depicts her characters; makes some critics call her "D.H Lawrence of the black psyche"[5]. In the *Encyclopedia of Race and Racism*, Kevin O. Cockley defines internalized racism as "the degree to which members of ethnic and racial minority groups agree with negative racist stereotypes attributed to their racial or ethnic minority groups, and consequently act on these beliefs." *(Cockley, 2008, p187)*. According to the definition given by Cockley, the internalization of racism is about the approval of the stereotypes that the dominant culture impose on blacks. This triggers off what Franz Fanon said about the psyche of blacks in a colonial context "the colonized internalizes this rejection of his culture, and begin to see his own culture as flawed, and is filled with shame and self-contempt "(Nayar, p. 47). Another concept related to the internalization of racism is interpellation, which was coined by Althusser. "interpellation describes a process by which the individual subjects come to internalize the dominant values of society...[like] Fanon's memory of being called a 'dirty nigger' in France, and the damaging impact this had on his sense of self and identity" (McLeod, p. 37).

Throughout the novel, various characters such as Pecola, Claudia as well as Cholly experience the internalization of racism in different ways. These characters incarnate what W.E.B Du Bois calls "double consciousness". In his *The Souls of Black Folk*, Bu Bois defines double consciousness as the "sense of looking at one's self through the eyes of other ... one ever

---

[5] Denard, Carolyn C. Ed. *Toni Morrison: conversations.* Schappell, Elissa. "Toni Morrison: The Art of Fiction". University of Mississippi. 2008

feels his two-ness, -- an American, a Negro; two souls, two thoughts, two unreconciled strivings; two warring ideals in one dark body" (Du Bois p. 5). Thus, double consciousness results in a crisis at the level of identity moving toward a postmodern fragmented self. In a foreword to her novel, *The Bluest Eye*, Morrison writes,

> I knew that some victims of powerful self-loathing turn out to be dangerous, violent, reproducing the enemy who has humiliated them over and over. Others surrender their identity; melt into a structure that delivers the strong persona they lack. Most others, however, grow beyond it. But there are some who collapse, silently, anonymously, with no voice to express or acknowledge it. They are invisible. The death of self-esteem can occur quickly, easily in children. *(The Bluest Eye, Foreword)*

When Morrison was writing her novel, she was aware about the consequences of racial shame especially on young black characters such as Pecola and Claudia. Some victims of racism resist the white ideologies and stereotypes. However, others internalize them,

> Morrison's treatment of racial shame in the novel enables her readers not only to unearth the significant psychological impact of Pecola and Claudia perceiving themselves as racially inferior, Pecola and Claudia are two of the most important vehicles Morrison employs for discussing salient issues about race. *(Maurice, 2011, p798)*

Pecola and Claudia remain the most important characters through which Morrison uncovers the issue of internalized racism. On the one hand, Pecola has been carrying the burden of racial shame on her shoulders since the beginning of the novel until she becomes mad. After her father has raped her, Pecola goes pregnant to see Soaphead Church whom claims himself a spiritualist in order to give her blues eyes, "I can't go to school no more. And I thought maybe you could help me." "Help you how? Tell me. Don't be frightened." "My eyes." "What about your eyes?" "I want them blue."*(The Bluest Eye, p174);* Undoubtedly, Pecola is very tired of bearing the heavy ideologies and stereotypes of the dominant culture. Moreover, her racial shame has increased after her father rapes her. Pecola's self-hatred makes her long for blues eyes because they will cure her racial shame,

> Pecola imagines that she can cure her ugliness—that is, her racial shame—only if she is miraculously granted the same blue eyes that little white girls possess. As Morrison describes the racial self-loathing of Pecola, she dramatizes the devastating impact of racial contempt on her shame-vulnerable character who has so internalized white contempt for her Blackness that she desires blue eyes so others will love and accept her. *(Bouson, 2003, p305)*

Pecola hates herself because of her race. According to her, blackness is disgusting. Thus, she wishes if only she is white. Whiteness will make her visible in school, street and even in her house. Pecola is convinced that she is inherently ugly. Consequently, she is psychologically wounded as Panlay argues, "The reason American blacks are psychologically wounded, argues West (1993a), is because they are convinced that their representations in the dominant discourse by white dominators are true." *(Panlay, 2016, p75)*. Pecola's encounter with a group of black boys is another exemplification of her racial shame, "Pecola is also shamed by a group of Black boys who circle her in the school playground, holding her at bay... By humiliating Pecola, as the narrative makes clear, the boys express their deep-rooted contempt for their own Black identity *(Bouson, 2003, p305)*. After Claudia and Frieda had left school with Maureen Peal, they found a group of black boys circling Pecola. They humiliated her with racial insults, "They danced a macabre ballet around the victim, whom, for their own sake, they were prepared to sacrifice to the flaming pit. 'Black e mo Black e moYa daddy sleeps nekked. Stch ta tastch ta tastach ta tatatata'. Pecola edged around the circle crying. She had dropped he notebook, and covered her eyes with her hands." *(The Bluest Eye, p65-66)*. The act of crying illustrates Pecola's racial shame. Pecola totally believes the black boys insults. Besides, it is worth to note that even the boys who had humiliated Pecola were themselves black. By doing so, Morrison shows how racial self-contempt is internalized and directed toward other black children as Morrison states,

> They had extemporized a verse made up of two insults about matters over which the victim had no control: the color of her skin and speculations on the sleeping habits of an adult, wildly fitting in its incoherence. That they themselves were black or that their own father had similarly relaxed habits was irrelevant. It was their contempt for their own blackness that gave the first insult its teeth. *(The Bluest Eye, p65)*

The black boys are not the only ones who aim their self-hatred toward their fellow blacks. Cholly also directs his self-contempt toward Darlene: "Cholly, moving faster, looked at Darlene. He hated her. He almost wished he could do it—hard, long, and painfully, he hated her so much." *(The Bluest Eye, p149)*. After their humiliation by the white hunters, Cholly aims his self-shame toward Darlene. Cholly could not aim his self-hatred toward the white hunters for the reason that he is powerless in comparison with them. Besides, Cholly thinks that hating the white hunters is worthless as Furman states, "When the men leave in search of other prey, Cholly realizes that hating them is futile, and he decides instead to hate Darlene for witnessing his degradation. He could not protect her so he settles for despising her" (Furman, 1999 p. 17). On the other hand, Claudia internalizes the stereotypes that the dominant culture draws about beauty as well, "It was a small step to Shirley Temple. I learned much later to worship her, just as I learned to delight in cleanliness, knowing, even as I learned, that the change was adjustment without improvement. *(The Bluest eye, p23)*. After a long rejection of the racialized ideologies about beauty, Claudia decides to fake her love for Shirley Temple, a symbol of white beauty. Claudia fabricates her love only because her sense of shame is unsettled. However, deep down, Claudia rejects the ideologies of the white dominant culture.

The issue of internalized racism does not only affect Morrison's fictional characters such as Pecola, Claudia, and Cholly. It even haunts the psyche of the African American society as a whole as Stephanie Li claims, "Pecola's desire for blue eyes represents a pervasive self-hatred that affects the entire African American community." *(Li, 2010, p37)*. In his essay, *What 'The Bluest Eye' knows about them: Culture, Race, Identity*, Christopher Douglas refers to a Doll experiment that was developed by Kenneth Clark and Mamie Clark. In their experiment, the Clarks used dolls to test a group of sixteen black children in an interview in one of Clarendon County's segregated schools. The black children's task was to choose one of the two, brown or white colored dolls. The Clarks came up with the following:

> He discovered that "[t]en of the sixteen children said they preferred the white doll. Eleven of the children referred to the black doll as 'bad,' while nine said the white doll was 'nice.' Seven of the children pointed to the white doll when they were asked to choose the doll most like themselves.
> *(Douglas, 2007, p216)*

The Clarks' Doll experiment is a real testimony of the African American community's self-loathing. The predilection of the black children to the white doll confirms the idealization and beauty of whiteness. Concisely, the internalization of racism remains one the most complicated issues that affect the psyche of the black community. Toni Morrison's *The Bluest Eye* is one of the first novels that deals with this psychological issue but it is not the last.

5. Conclusion:

'Race' in *The Bluest Eye* remains an umbrella term that covers various issues such as racialized beauty, whiteness, racism as well as internalized racism. In *The Bluest Eye,* beauty is based on racialized characteristics imposed by the white dominant culture, which exclude African Americans from the realm of beauty. Beauty means whiteness. Therefore, numerous African American poets neutralized the standards of beauty by celebrating their black natural features throughout their literary works. Furthermore, "black is beautiful" slogan and the Afrocentric movement challenged Eurocentrism by taking into account the African and African American culture as well. Furthermore, whiteness in *The Bluest Eye* is ideal. To be white, means to be pure, clean and even beautiful. As a medium, the cinema plays a major role in disseminating the ideals of whiteness. Most of the actresses who appear in movies are whites. These white movie stars preoccupy the minds of various black characters to the extent that some of them compare the reflection of white beauty on the screen with their ugly dark skin. Whiteness is divine. Many people believe that God is white. Besides, throughout the American literary canon, several white American writers represent black characters with bad connotations. The misunderstanding of race has led many people to commit cruel acts throughout history. These people suppress the existence of some races for the reason that they are backward, barbaric, and even ugly. However, at the human level, we understand that all races are even. It is just a matter of difference. Throughout the novel, many white characters maltreat and even dehumanize blacks. Furthermore, whites take advantage of blacks economically. Capitalism divides the world of the novel into two social classes. The white high class and the black working class. Therefore, the nature of the exploitative economical system results in racism as well as classism. Internalized racism is one of the issues that still haunts the psyche of the black community. To a certain extent, African Americans agree on the white racial stereotypes. Thus, they are psychologically wounded. At any rate, through *The Bluest Eye,* Morrison tries to explain to the reader how one's race could lead to madness, self-hatred, marginalization and racial oppression. This is the aim of literature. It shares with us human values in order to reshape the concept of humanity. As an African American writer, Toni Morrison highly recognizes the black race. She sinks deep into the psyche of her fictional characters in order to show how they feel because of the nature of their race.

Work cited:

Angelou, Maya. *The complete collected poems of Maya Angelou.* Random House, 1994. PDF

Barthes, Roland. *Image, Music, Text.* Tran. Stephen Heath. Fontana Press. 1997. PDF

Beaulieu, Elizabeth Ann. Ed. *Writing African American Women: An Encyclopedia of Literature
    by and about Women of Color.* Olson, Debbie Clare. "Beauty". Greenwood Press. 2006. PDF

_____. Smith-Spears, RaShell R. *"Bennett, Gwendolyn B".* Greenwood Press. 2006. PDF

Beaulieu, Elizabeth Ann. Ed. *"The Toni Morrison".* Magill, E. David *"Whiteness".* Greenwood.
    2003. PDF

_____. Bouson, J. Brooks. "Shame" Greenwood. 2003. PDF

_____. Chandler, Gena Elise. *"Pauline Breedlove (The Bluest Eye).* Greenwood. 2003. PDF

Bloom, Harold. Ed. *Bloom's guides: Toni Morrison's The Bluest Eye.* "The story behind the
    story" InfoBase publishing, 2010. PDF

_____. Mbalia, Doreatha Drummond *"On Class versus Race as a Cause of Black
    Oppression"* InfoBase publishing, 2010. PDF

Bloom, Harold. Ed. *Bloom's Modern Critical Interpretations: Toni Morrison's The Bluest Eye –
    updated edition.* Fick, Thomas H. *"Toni Morrison's 'Allegory of the cave': Movies,
    Consumption and Platonic Realism in the Bluest Eye'.* InfoBase publishing, 2007. PDF

_____. Alexander, Allen *"The Fourth face: The Image of God in Toni Morrison's
    The Bluest Eye".* InfoBase publishing, 2007. PDF

_____. Douglas, Christopher. *"What 'The Bluest Eye' knows about them:
    Culture, Race, Identity".* InfoBase publishing, 2007. PDF

Bloom, Harold. Ed. *"Bloom's Modern Critical Views: Toni Morrison".* Bloom, Harold
    Introduction. Chelsea House, 2005. PDF

Blum, J. Edward & Harvey, Paul *"The Color of Christ: the Son of God and the Saga of Race in
    America".* Introduction: *"The holy face of race".* The University of North Carolina Press,
    2012. PDF

Craig, Maxine Leeds, *"Ain't I a Beauty Queen: Black Women, Beauty, and the politics of race".*
    "Contexts for the emergence of "Black is Beautiful". Oxford University Press. 2002. PDF

Douglass, Frederick. *"Narrative of the life of Frederick Douglass".* Dover Publications, Inc. 1995

Du Bois, W.E.B. *The Souls of Black Folk.* Yale university press. 1903

Edgar, Andrew and Sedgwick, Peter. *Cultural Theory: Key Thinkers.* Routeldge. 2002

Ellison, Ralph. *"Invisible man"*. *"Prologue"*. Random House, 1947. PDF

Furman, Jan. *Toni Morrison's Fiction*. *"Black Girlhood and Black Womanhood, the Bluest Eye and Sula"*. University of South Carolina Press, 1999. PRINT

Li, Stephanie. *"Toni Morrison: A biography"*. *"Early Literary Career"*. Greenwood Press, 2010.

Lister, Rachel. *Reading Toni Morrison*. "The Bluest Eye". The Pop Lit Book Club, 2009. PDF

_____. "Today's Issue in Toni Morrison's work". The Pop Lit Book Club 2009. PDF

McClinton-Temple, Jennifer. Ed. *"Encyclopedia of Themes in Literature"*. Daniels, Antonio Maurice. *"The Bluest Eye"*. Facts on Files, Inc. 2011. PDF

McLeod, John. *Beginning Postcolonialism*. Manchester UP. 2000. PDF

Morrison, Toni. *Playing in the Dark: Whiteness and the Literary Imagination*. Vintage books. 1993. PDF

_____. *The Bluest Eye a Novel*. Vintage eBooks, 2007. PDF

Moore, John Hartwell. Ed. *Encyclopedia of Race and Racism*. Moore, John Hartwell. Introduction. McMillan 2008. PDF

_____. Cokley, O. Kevin. *"Internalized Racism"*. McMillan 2008. PDF

Mills, Sara. *Michel Foucault*. Routledge. 2003

Nayar. Pramod. K. *Frantz Fanon*. Routledge. 2003

Gillespie, Carmen. *"Critical Companion to Toni Morrison: A Literary Reference to Her Life and Work"*. *"The Bluest Eye"*. Facts on File, 2008. PDF

Tally, Justine. Ed. *The Cambridge Companion to Toni Morrison*. Suranyi, Agnes *"The Bluest Eye and Sula: black female experience from childhood to womanhood"* 2007. Cambridge UP

The World Book Encyclopedia. Garn, M. Stanley. *"Races, Human"*. World book Inc. 1985. PRINT

_____. Pettigrew, Thomas. *"Racism"* World book Inc. 1985. PRINT

Smith, Jessie Carney, Ed. *"Encyclopedia of African American popular culture"*. Knight, Gladys L. *"Afrocentric Movement"*. Greenwood. 2011. PDF

Perry, Richard J. *"Race" and Racism: The Development of Modern Racism in America. "Race": fact or artifact?* Palgrave, 2007. PDF

Panlay, Suriyan. *"Racism in contemporary African American Children's and Young Adult Literature"*. Introduction. *"Wounds of internalized racism: Business As usual"* Palgrave Macmillan. 2016. PDF

Webliography:

McGruder, Aaron, and Clattenburg, Mike. *"Black Jesus"*. Imdb, 7. Aug. 2014. <Http: //www.imdb.com/title/tt358982/>. Web

Madonna. *"Like a Prayer"*. YouTube, 26. Oct. 2006, <http: //www.youtube.com/watch?v=79fzeNUqQbQ>. Web

Bennet, Gwendolyn B. *"To a Dark Girl"*. <Http: //m.poemhunter.com/poem/to-a-dark-girl/>. Web

Parini, Jay. *"What's wrong with Black Jesus?"* CNN, 30, July 2014. <Http:
//edition.cnn.com/2014/07/29/opinion/parini-black-jesus/index>

Bharati, Megha & Joshi, L.M. *"Race, class and gender bias as reflected by in Toni Morrison's novel
The Bluest Eye"*. Journal of literature, Culture and Media studies, 2009. PDF <Http:
//www.inflibnet.ac.in/ojs/index.php/JLCMS/article/view/4/3>

Denard, Carolyn C. Ed. "Toni Morrison: conversations". Schappell, Elissa. *"Toni Morrison:
The Art of Fiction"*. University of Mississippi. 2008. <http:
//books.google.co.ma/books/about/Toni_Morrison.html?id=eV9_8v4pTsC&redir_esc=y>. Web